The Stanley Museum celebrates F.O. Stanley's impact on Estes Park and Colorado, and his use of the automobile to move tourism out of the 19th century.

The Museum also honors Stanley's love of Estes Park and his investment in its future—roads, transportation, bank, water company, power company, hotel, recreation, and more—all fundamentals that helped Estes Park lead the development of Colorado's tourism.

The Stanleys'—F.O.'s and his wife, Flora's—love of Estes Park is so enduring, it lives on in these stories today.

THE STANLEY MUSEUM'S MISSION

The Stanley Museum
keeps and shares the traditions of
Yankee ingenuity and creativity
as exemplified by the Stanley family
in order to inspire these values
in children and adults.

INSTITUTIONAL VISION & VALUES

The Stanley Museum shall be for all an
institution of learning
dedicated to a celebration of
Yankee ingenuity
as exemplified by the Stanley twins,
Freelan Oscar and Francis Edgar,
their sister Chansonetta Stanley Emmons,
and their American contemporaries.

The Stanley Museum shall strive to
preserve the history of their achievements
and the artifacts and technology
relevant to them for the purpose of
arousing in the public pride of heritage
and promoting those values most cherished
and valuable in the American experience –
Family Excellence, Integrity, Creativity, a
Love of Learning, Tenacity,
and Good Citizenship.

Adopted Unanimously October 14, 2000

STANLEY GHOST STORIES

Edited by Susan S. Davis

for

The Stanley Museum

Kingfield, Maine

THE STANLEY MUSEUM

PO Box 77, Kingfield, Maine 04947
Telephone: 207-265-2729 Facsimile 207-265-4700
E-mail: maine@stanleymuseum.org

Stanley Ghost Stories
Edited by Susan S. Davis for the Stanley Museum

First Edition June 2005
Revised Edition June 2012

ISBN: 978-1-886727-12-0

Photograph on Front Cover:
  Stanley Hotel from the archives of the Stanley Museum, Kingfield,
  Maine
Cover Design: Carrabassett Marketing & Printing, North Anson,
  Maine
Photographs on pages 12, 13, 20, 22, 23, 24, 30, 32 © 2004 Chris
  Bechard, Alpenglow Media

TABLE OF CONTENTS

ACKNOWLEDGEMENTS

The Stanley Museum's Ghost Story Tours of the Stanley Hotel were started in 1998 by museum site manager, Marty Yochum, now Marty Casey. Subsequent managers have included Elle DeLeone (the only Stanley Museum staff person to personally experience these spirits), Kevin Croghan and Maureen Corey. Ghost Story tour guides have included Gina Beisheim, Tom Danton, John Erickson, Serena Fridh, Kurtis Kelly, Cyndi Ray, Diego Reyes, and a long list of part-time volunteers and staff. The stories have been collected over eight years by Stanley Museum staff, and friends who have shared them.

In alphabetical order, we would like to thank those to whom we can attach specific stories. We have made every effort to find these people to get permission to use their stories, and hereby apologize to any we have missed: Chris Bechard, Gary and Kelly Brown, Marty Yochum Casey, Maureen Corey, John Craigmile, Tom Danton, Dawn from housekeeping, Carrisa Delisse, John Michael Grace, Derek Key, Paul Klasky, Jason Kurtis, Mark Lorenz, Karen Lynch, Paula Peat Page Martin, Charlotte Riley, Will and Ann Rice, Andrew Smith, Tim Stolz, Elizabeth (& John) Whisler, and Darlene Wilson.

For the Alpenglow Media photographs taken January 18, 2004, Chris Bechard used a Nikon D100 camera on a tripod with 10-second exposures @ f/5.6 with an 80 mm (28-80mm zoom) Nikkor-G lens and circular polarizer filter and a film speed setting at ISO/200. All of Chris's photographs were taken following staff reports of a period of out-of-the-ordinary activity.

Thank you to our editors: Gina Beisheim, Jeniffer Cooley, Caprissa Frawley, Kurtis Kelly, Dottie Nobles and John White.

Some of our best stories have come from two Stanley Hotel Alumni get-togethers held in February and March 2005. Demand suggests we do them again. If you have stories you would like to share, please call to tell us, or write them up with as much detail as to time, place and names as possible, and send them along, with permission to use. Please include detailed contact information, that we might call for clarification to assure we relate these experiences correctly.

There appear to be volumes of stories, for those interested!

Susan S. Davis for The Stanley Museum, June 2005
Kingfield, Maine — F.O.'s birthplace and, with Flora, burial place;
Estes Park, Colorado — the Stanleys' favorite haunt.

INTRODUCTION

Some of our stories are at least 25 years old; some are very recent. There are simply too many to ignore. Some may be aprocryphal, taking on lives of their own, some have been handed down essentially without change. We have made every effort to separate fact from fiction. There is no doubt much of this happened, and is still happening. Some have nice neat beginnings and endings—many do not. They come in many varieties, making it difficult to organize them. By loose categories, there are the following:

1) **Sounds only:** babies crying, walking and running in the hallways, bouncing on beds;

2) **Movement with no visible agent:** the elevator moving on its own, doors and windows opening and shutting; parties heard but not seen;

3) **Visible representations seen only in photographs:** orbs, mist, ectoplasm (human shapes);

4) **Visible appearances seen by individuals:** men, women and children, always dressed in early 20th-century style clothing; parties seen and heard;

5) **Physical:** spirits passing through a person, experience of extreme warmth or cold, electrical shocks.

For simplicity purposes, we will organize them by location.

Those who have studied the paranormal have also organized the types of appearances spirits make into three kinds: mist, orbs and ectoplasm. The first two forms are reasonably self-explanatory. Ectoplasm seems a scientific word for such an ethereal, aerie phenomenon, when mist starts taking a recognizable shape, a human form.

Ectoplasm is a subtle substance on the boundary between physical and nonphysical that, according to researchers into Spiritualism, exudes from the body of certain mediums. This quasi-physical material is transformed into the substance that is perceived during so-called materialization phenomena, when limbs, faces, or even whole bodies of spirits appear in séances (Lewis, p. 117).

Ectoplasm can be warm or cold, can be weighed, and often feels like rubber or dough to the touch. It is frequently white, and is said to smell like ozone. Its structure varies widely, from a cloudy mist, to solid rods, to net-like membrane (Lewis, p. 117).

F.O. and Flora Stanley in a 1902 Stanley steam runabout, photographed near Boston, Massachusetts, on August 12, 1902, just months before F.O. was stricken with tuberculosis and forced to move west to Colorado. On August 31, 1899, the Stanleys drove an earlier, more primitive version of this car to the summit of Mount Washington in New Hampshire, proudly accomplishing an automotive first.

From the Stanley Museum archives

UNTITLED POEM
by Flora J. T. Stanley

Among the leaves
The sad wind grieves
The rain falls drearily
The branches sway
In a weird way
The clouds move wearily

The ghostly rap
And knock and tap
Of branches and wind and rain
Call answering ghosts
From Memory's hosts
I strive to stay in vain.

A Mellow note
From feathered throat
Falls with the falling rain

Above the grief
Of wind and leaf
Drips down the sweet refrain.

So amid the ghosts
Of Memory's hosts
A living hope appear'd
And from her throat
A silv'ry note
Falls with the falling tears.

Oft in the dark
The firefly's spark
Will cheer the traveler's way
And amid the rain
Thy sweet refrain
Sends music through the day.

Although most of our stories are about happenings, there are some stories about form. Cameras, especially digital, but even regular 35-mm cameras, have captured mist, orbs and ectoplasm that those holding the camera did not see.

It has become clear to us that spirits show up where they are welcome, believed in, sometimes sought out. Museum site manager Kevin Croghan's mantra, "Whether you believe in them and are scared by them is your choice," fits here.

FLORA J. T. STANLEY

Flora Jane Record Tileston, later Mrs. Freelan Oscar (F.O.) Stanley, 1848-1939, was born in Maine and died at her home in Estes Park. In *Untitled Poem*, she writes: *The ghostly rap... Call answering ghosts From Memory's hosts I strive to stay in vain*, Flora almost predicts her appearances, the most documented of all ghost stories at the Stanley Hotel. At last, her heavy "mortal coil" has been shed, and she can wander the halls and rooms of her beautiful Stanley Hotel, no longer encumbered by the debilitating blindness of her later years. (She may also have suffered from what we call today manic depression or bipolar disorder.) As a member of the Estes Park community, she was active in what became the Estes Park Women's Club. Curiously, the club's most successful fundraiser was Flora's program: she dressed as a gypsy and told people's fortunes.

Since her death, Flora has appeared often at the hotel, mostly in the lobby and the Music Room. Visions of her are characterized by her high, white lace collar. She has been seen on the grand staircase, either following people up, or coming down by herself, possibly standing behind an unsuspecting girl, perhaps even at the front desk.

In 1995, when ABC was at the Stanley Hotel filming *The Shining*, they created a fake bloodstain on the floor. Flora's picture reportedly flew off the wall onto the stain. Was she saying she was unhappy with such an impropriety at her hotel? Did it really happen that way?

F.O. & FLORA STANLEY IN ESTES PARK

The Stanley Hotel opened June 22, 1909, built by Maine-born Massachusetts resident, Freelan Oscar Stanley. With his loving—and unusual—wife Flora, F.O. Stanley had arrived in Estes Park June 30,

1903, in search of health. F.O. had tuberculosis, and in those days, the clean, dry air of the Colorado Rockies was a well known tonic for the disease.

The Stanleys had no intentions beyond health when they arrived. Fate met capacity, though, when this "wealthy eastern industrialist" came to town. His health returned, they became summer residents, and in 1907, a Greeley, Colorado, irrigationist named Burton Davis Sanborn, asked Stanley's help to purchase 6,000 acres from the Irish Earl, Lord Dunraven.

Stanley was already embarked on what became a string of contributions to the town of Estes Park. With masterful community building, he turned Estes into an economic powerhouse of tourism well before Colorado gave up on mining as its primary economy. Roads, transportation, water, power, sewer, banking, then golf, streams restocked with fish, meadows with elk, Rocky Mountain National Park, and a rodeo ground—all supported not only Stanley's grand hotel, but the community as a whole.

When the Stanleys arrived in 1903, all Estes Park accommodations—from cabins like the first ones they stayed in, to the hotels and guest ranches—were rustic. At the end of their first year, F.O. and Flora built their own home in the Eastern Georgian Colonial Revival style they were used to in Massachusetts.

The Stanley home in Estes Park, built in 1903-1904, on Wonderview Avenue, Route 36 By-Pass. This is still a private home.   *From the Stanley Museum archives*

When Stanley agreed to take part in the Sanborn deal, he saw an opportunity to bring variety in the accommodations room stock, to build a hotel in the same style as his home that would be the largest and grandest in the town, indeed, in the entire state of Colorado at that time. In one lavish $500,000 stroke, Stanley expanded the room inventory not only in number but in variety. Now, an even broader spectrum of people—with money—had a choice of accommodations.

GHOSTS AND SPIRITS AT THE STANLEY HOTEL

F.O. and Flora Stanley were very happy with their life in Estes Park and at the Stanley Hotel. Their guests also enjoyed their stays at their hotel, many of them coming for the entire summer with children and staff. Herein lies the connection of spirits, or ghosts, at the Stanley Hotel: spirits are energy, and energy shows up where it is strongest, often happiest. Both F.O. and Flora have been sighted frequently by trustworthy sources long since their physical departure. Many other spirits have also been seen or experienced, heard or photographed.

The Stanley Hotel has no dark history. No-one has been murdered there, the few deaths recorded have been of natural causes. All first-person reports of guests and staff and their times at the Stanley and in Estes Park long-past have been full of fond memories. Whether summer vacations, weddings, birthdays, anniversaries, or other special occasions, time spent in Estes Park at the Stanley Hotel has been some of the happiest in many visitors' lives.

Based on personal reports of such special times, nothing scary preceded Stephen King (see p.1), and nothing scary has happened since. Reports of anything even approaching unpleasant are minor when compared to the many reports of mischievous attention getters, helpful antics—doors opening by themselves—or simply random happenings.

We will report all we know well enough to tell.

We are not ghost busters or spirit chasers. We are simply telling the stories we've heard in the context of the Estes Park Stanley experience. Let us start with an in depth look at Stephen King's role in the Stanley story, in great part to clear up the many inaccuracies and some of the stories that seem to have taken on a life of their own.

By the way—Stephen King and F.O. Stanley are both from Maine.

The Stanley Hotel, Estes Park, Colorado, designed and built by F.O. Stanley. This classic photo was taken some time after the hotel was completed, circa 1910-1912.
                                        From the Stanley Museum archives

STEPHEN KING AND *The Shining*

Stephen King's *The Shining* was inspired by a night at the Stanley Hotel in 1974.

In late September that year, Stephen King and his wife Tabitha checked in to the Stanley Hotel on what proved to be the hotel's last night of the season—the Stanley did not become a year-round hotel until 1984. They were the only guests (King, p. 61), and almost couldn't check in because all the charge slips but one American Express form had been sent to the business office in Denver (Beahm, p. 69). Since King had the American Express card, all was saved—in 1982, he even starred in a Celebrity Series ad for American Express, adding emphasis to the claim that he "never leaves home without it."

The Kings stayed in room 217—not because the hotel knew who he was, but simply because it made sense to give the best room in the house to the only guests. They ate dinner in the hotel's Colorado Restaurant, after which his wife retired. King, however, went back downstairs and had a drink in the bar served by a bartender named Grady. Afterwards, he wandered the halls, and by the time he got back to the room and noticed the claw-foot tub in the bathroom, his story was formed.

King had been stuck on a story line "loosely based on the Patricia Hearst-SLA [Symbionese Liberation Army] business... (that) just wasn't marching" (King, p. 61). He'd also been playing with an idea for a book called *Darkshine*. He "wondered what would happen if you had a little boy who was sort of a receptor, or maybe even a psychic amplifier. And I wanted to take a little kid with his family and put them someplace, cut off, where spooky things would happen. I sort of wanted it to be Disney World—Goofy's coming to kill you..." (p. 68, Beahm).

But it wouldn't work. Not until he stayed that night at the Stanley and changed the venue to an old hotel. "He imagined the fire hoses coming alive, thumping across the carpet. 'By then,' King recalled, 'whatever it is that makes you want to make things up... was turned on. I was scared, but I loved it'" (Beahm, p. 69).

King was once asked if he had ever written anything really scary that kept him up all night. Once again, he referred to *The Shining*: "Yeah. Not very often, though, because a lot of the time, you feel like you've got it in the palm of your hand.... But sometimes I think it gets out. The worst one was the tub thing in *The Shining*.... It wasn't too bad

1

when I wrote it; all at once it was just there.... But on the rewrite, as I got closer to that point, I would say to myself, eight days to the tub, and then six days to the tub. And then one day it was *the tub today*. When I went down to the typewriter that day I felt frightened and my heart was beating too fast and I felt the way you do when you have to make a big presentation, or when something's going to happen. And I was scared. I did the best job I could with it, but I was glad when it was over" (King, p. 249).

The Shining worked so well, as a matter of fact, that he commented, "I never have written a book that went so smoothly.... The story unspooled without a hitch or a snag" (King, p. 62). When his Doubleday editor, Bill Thompson, finally saw it, it also proved to be "of all the novels I've published... the one that required the least rewriting" (King, p. 66). It's tempting to ponder just how much the Stanley Hotel did to inspire this novel.

Another strange twist in the novel that King may or may not have been responsible for showed up in the end of the book for this reader (writers are often mediums for stories rather than creators, as King suggested in his mention of the tub above). When Dick Halloran, the chef, loses his summer job because the Overlook burns, he finds a job in Rangeley, Maine, in a sporting camp about 30 miles from the center of town. Hmmm. That also happens to be approximately how far Kingfield is from Rangeley as the bird flies. Kingfield is the birth and burial site of—F.O. Stanley.

The family was staying in Boulder in 1974 so that King could write a book in a new locale—*Carrie* and *'Salem's Lot*, both sited in Maine, were already in print. With a whole story now in place with a new, Colorado, setting, King rented a room in downtown Boulder, and by January, the first draft of the book was virtually done, by then under the name, *The Shine*.

Before Doubleday released the book in January 1977, Warner Bros. bought the rights, with Stanley Kubrick and Jack Nicholson in mind. But Warner Bros. didn't like the title. "They wanted it retitled *The Shining*, because "shine" is a pre-World War II pejorative for black, as in 'Hey, shoeshine boy,' (because) one of the main characters (was) a black cook named Dick Hallorann.

"Someone in Warner Bros.' title department," King goes on, "felt that people would think the title a half-satirical gibe at my black character. So we changed it to *The Shining* (the original title had been

2

suggested by a John Lennon song, 'Instant Karma,' the chorus of which goes, 'We all shine on... like the moon and the stars and the sun...'), which I have learned to live with but which still strikes me as rather unwieldy and thudding" (King, p. 67).

The Shining turned into King's first hardcover bestseller, contributing no doubt to the excitement and anticipation for Kubrick's movie, which arrived two and a half years later, in June 1979. According to his friend, Chris Chesley, King "liked what the director had done, but... (it) wasn't his book—it was Kubrick's movie" (Beahm, p. 88).

Kubrick determined that the movie could not be filmed at the Stanley Hotel site because there was not enough snow, and the town encroached on the hotel too closely for the distance shots. The film was shot primarily in England, where Kubrick lived, with a 15-second exterior shot of Timberline Lodge on Mt. Hood in Oregon. This is of course the answer to one of the most frequently asked questions "Where is the hedge maze?" In England, of course.

In 1995, Stephen King and ABC teamed up to create a three-segment mini-series of The Shining, filmed at the Stanley Hotel and in studios in Denver. The timing was perfect for the hotel, King got to come back to the Stanley and ABC got a ready-made set—almost. The ABC producer walked into the white, plaster Georgian Colonial lobby of the Stanley and, declaring that 'this would NOT do,' ordered it changed to its current fake-wood look, referred to properly as faux bois (fake wood in French). In fact, the only wood in the entire lobby and MacGregor dining room is that of door and window frames, easily seen on close examination.

Stanley Hotel ownership changed through a bankruptcy action in May 1995. The new owners welcomed the use of the hotel for a movie while it gathered itself to embark later on what turned into a multi-million dollar renovation (upgrades are still taking place). Thus, ABC had remarkable free rein in changing things to suit its needs. Who would mind new paint and interior decorations the owners didn't need to fund?

King worked on the production of the TV movie, from the script to a cameo appearance as band director at the ball. The mini-series is not as well known as the Kubrick movie, but the fan base of both range from mild to extreme, bringing the Stanley Hotel, called in the book The Overlook, right along with it in popularity. The book's disclaimer reads:

**Some of the most beautiful resort hotels in the world
are located in Colorado, but the hotel in these pages
is based on none of them. The Overlook and
the people associated with it exist wholly
within the author's imagination.**

True enough, for none of the spirits reported to have been seen or experienced in the Stanley Hotel are mean enough to have acted as King's did.

Early drawing of the Stanley Hotel, of the time from which most of the spirits sighted today may have come.   *From the Stanley Museum archives*

THE MAIN BUILDING

The centerpiece of the Stanley Hotel is the westernmost building in the four-building sweep, rising from below with one story at the Carriage House, two stories at the Concert Hall/Casino, three stories at the Manor House and finally four stories topped by the tower in this building. Early brochures talked of The Stanley Hotels in the plural. This main building was only a summer hotel from 1909 to 1984, always the first to be filled. The Manor House was built the second year based on need determined the first year, and to provide spring and fall accommodations—it is sometimes called the Winter Hotel. As one might expect, most stories of spirits come from the main building, which has always had the heaviest traffic.

FIRST FLOOR

MACGREGOR DINING ROOM

The MacGregor Dining Room on the main floor is named for one of Estes Park's early ranching settlers, known for his toll road into Estes, and for defending his land against the Irish Earl, Lord Dunraven, who's portrait curiously holds a place of honor immediately outside the dining room. It is the hotel's formal dining room, used today only

Stanley Hotel MacGregor Dining Room c. 1910, showing waiters assigned to each table for the duration of a guest's stay.   *From the Stanley Museum archives*

5

for special occasions, replaced for regular dining by today's Cascade Bar and Dining Room. In the beginning, this dining room served guests on the American Plan—three meals a day. Before its allocation for special events only, it served hotel clientele and the public a standard, often gourmet, a la carte menu.

This room was the scene in June 1911 of an accident that we think might be the source of many of today's spirit experiences. The accident originated directly above the dining room in the famous Room 217. Look for the story when we get to the second floor.

This room was used for the famous ball scene in the ABC miniseries of *The Shining*. Today the pilasters and plaster covered steel beams still sport the faux bois look, rather than the correct white of the building's architectural style. The stage in the room is an extension of the original piano proscenium, built out by ABC for the band. Stephen King made his cameo appearance here in the TV movie.

December 30, 1970, housekeeper Arty Roberts was to clean the dance floor in the MacGregor Room for the special New Year's dance for which the Stanley opened every winter. She entered the MacGregor Room, and it felt like she was entering another time. People were dressed in period dress: long skirts, high collars, tuxedos. Concerned, she turned around and walked back to the night clerk at the front desk to ask her what was going on. The clerk was eating her dinner and appeared not only not to notice Arty, but apparently not to notice any of the noise emanating from the MacGregor. Arty returned to the room, where she went about her business. She did not feel threatened by the room full of spirits, and they appeared oblivious to her scrubbing.

DUNRAVEN / CASCADES

The Cascades used to be called the Dunraven Bar & Grille. This room was added onto the present hotel, probably in the 1950s.

In November 2002, the staff person working at the front desk asked the night bartender if he would please stop stacking the chairs on the bar, done so that the cleaning staff could vacuum. The night before, he had walked into the bar after closing and the chairs began to fall off one by one in a manner that frightened him beyond words.

Sometime in the 1980s, pianist Tim Stolz was finishing up his set for the night in the Dunraven. There were a few couples still finishing a late dinner. The pianist planned to finish his last set with

"Amazing Grace." Just then, a middle-aged man and older woman, his mother, arrived and took a seat near the piano. The pianist thought to ask the woman if she had a request for his last song. He stood up and walked over to speak with her, upon which she requested "Danny Boy," which he returned and played.

He then felt inspired to play "Amazing Grace" anyway, which he did beautifully, personally so moved that tears streamed down his face as he played. The performance received an ovation, whereupon the older woman stood up and announced to the room that "Amazing Grace" was her late husband's favorite song. Then she and her companion left.

A couple sitting nearby appeared to be very alarmed, the woman's face extremely pale. The man rose from his table and asked Tim, in a shaky voice, how he was able to do that. The pianist didn't know what he was talking about. The man then explained that, when Tim had crossed the room to talk to the woman, an older man followed him very closely. Then, when he began playing "Amazing Grace," the man stood behind him, with a hand on his shoulder. Tim got up to try to find the man and woman who had just left, but they were nowhere to be seen.

LOBBY

The Lobby, its original white plaster also painted faux bois as in the MacGregor Dining Room, is the scene of many ghostly experiences and appearances. Whether F.O. and Flora are seen checking on staff, standing at the front desk, walking down the stairs, or the room suddenly becomes empty when full, there are many stories about this part of the hotel.

Sometime during 2003, Carissa Delisse, night clerk at the front desk, felt someone looking at her or over her shoulder as she was working. She looked up, but saw no-one. It happened again; again, she looked up and saw no-one. Soon again, she felt the presence, but this time she raised her eyes only, rather than her head, and there was F.O. Stanley standing at the counter watching her. When she raised her head to look in his eyes, F.O. faded away.

In February of 1984, at 10:30 at night in the small alcove behind the front desk, bellman Mark Lorenz heard seven steps come from the Dunraven Bar, (now Cascades) and stop. He stepped forward to the front desk, and in the window glass of the front porch, he saw

The lobby in Stanley's day, looking west toward the MacGregor Dining Room. The front desk is in the alcove just past the stairs. The hallway to the Dunraven Bar &
Grille of later years is to the left at the end of the lobby.
From the Stanley Museum archives.

the reflection of a woman with an off-the-shoulder gown, hair piled high, with ringlets. The outfit was a cream-colored southern belle gown. Mark moved quickly out the door into the lobby and in several broad strides, he was in the entryway to the Dunraven. No one was there. He checked the MacGregor Dining Room, the front porch, and when he opened the door to the Dunraven Bar, everyone there turned to look at him. Being winter, many were wearing ski clothes with big fuzzy boots (strange what you notice!). He went to the other exit of the bar, looked at the top of the basement stairs and saw and heard nothing.

In 1995 during the filming of *The Shining*, Paula Peat Page, Head of Sales for the Stanley, was helping prepare for a group coming for dinner in the Music Room. The ABC crew was running late filming a segment in the Piñon Room, and agreed to help when they were done so that preparation time for hotel staff was cut down and they could finish filming. Something was missing for the buffet tables, so Paula offered to go to the kitchen at the other end of the Lobby to get it.

The Lobby as it appears today. Note the bright spot above the stair railing. Perhaps F.O. or Flora coming down the stairs...?   *Stanley Museum photo*

She took off across the Lobby, and heard her name called behind her. She turned back, and no-one was there. In fact absolutely no-one was there—the Lobby, bustling with film crew and hotel staff bare seconds before, was completely empty. She shook her head in bewilderment, but being efficient and unflappable Paula, she turned back to her task and retrieved the missing items from the kitchen. When she returned to the Lobby, it was back to normal, bustling with people and activity. As she got back to her friend at the table, Paula asked her what had happened, why had everyone disappeared. Her friend assured her, nothing had happened, they had all been there the whole time.

On August 23, 2004, after taking the Stanley Museum's history tour, a young lady sat down in one of the armchairs in the Lobby. Her friend took her picture, and when they developed it, the picture appeared to have something that appeared directly behind her as a form. Looking carefully at the image, one can almost imagine the fold of a garment like those worn by Flora Stanley.

ELEVATOR

In King's novel, the elevator takes on a sinister note. Although not sinister in real life, there are stories.

In 1983 Mark Lorenz, then in the engineering department, lived in the hotel, often the only person on the property outside of working staff. The security officer, Edgar Allen Poe III (no joke!), always took the elevator to the fourth floor to do his rounds at night if there were no guests, so Mark was familiar with the sound of the elevator stopping, the door opening, the door closing and the elevator moving to each floor as the officer did his rounds from top to bottom. This time, the elevator stopped at each of the floors, but the door never opened. He found the elevator on the third floor outside his room with no one in it or anywhere near, took it to the lobby, locked it and left, realizing no one had been there to operate it.

Also in the 1980s, John Grace was working alone nights on the set for an Estes Park Fine Arts Guild theater production of a murder mystery in the MacGregor Dining Room. On the fourth night, he heard something in the lobby. When he went to check, it was the elevator, which then stopped at the lobby level and opened, with nobody in it. Knowing it was only manually operated, when no-one stepped out, he freaked out, gathered up his tools and nearly flew out of the building. He admitted that it didn't help that he was reading *The Shining* at home nights during that period working alone at the Stanley.

CHRYSALIS GIFT SHOP

Today's Chrysalis Gift Shop used to be the Lady's Writing Parlor. It was fashionable in those days for women to keep journals, write letters and cards, and in Flora's case to write articles often published in magazines of the day. When the men were playing golf or otherwise together, the women might stay inside in the morning or afternoon to write.

In August 2000, during a tour, the guide was explaining how ghosts like to play with light and water, at which point the lights in the closed gift shop flashed on and off. (We have even caught the owner of the hotel helping to set the scene of a ghostly encounter, so we can never be sure that this was not set up.)

MUSIC ROOM

This room is the site of the Stanley Hotel's best known and best documented haunting. To this day, people hear, or see, Flora Stanley at her piano, or most recently, near the piano. Knowing the history will help explain what happens here, and why. The Steinway grand piano that graces the small stage in the alcove was F.O. Stanley's gift to his wife Flora on the opening of the Stanley Hotel, June 22, 1909.

The Music Room, perhaps the most beautiful room in the hotel, fits the Stanley family—even in their private homes in Newton, Massachusetts, their music rooms were elegantly appointed, often the largest as well as most stunning rooms in their homes. Interest in music was not uncommon in the day, but the Stanleys took it further than most, from building fine violins, to owning the best pianos, studying voice, even composing music. The Concert Hall (originally called the Casino, meaning entertainment, not gambling), one of the four primary buildings of the hotel, was designed for music, and in fact is the only other space on the property with the same amount of architectural detailing, a sure sign of F.O. Stanley's artistic investment in music, and thus in these spaces.

In the early 1970s, the Stanley Hotel was in the most rundown condition of its history. People were literally backing up to the building and taking furniture away by the truckload. The Steinway was moved into hiding by its owners for its protection. It returned in 1976 when the Normalis finalized their purchase of the hotel. Most of the stories of hearing it played started after that. We have chosen to interpret that as a statement by Flora that she is glad to have her piano back. The music is often Strauss, Flora's favorite composer. There is also the strong smell of roses in the room, Flora's favorite flower, and perhaps perfume.

In 1976, night auditor and clerk, Carol O'Dell, heard music playing from the front desk. She walked across the Lobby to the door of the Music Room, where the music was coming from, and saw the keys of the piano move, but no-one there. Many have reported hearing music, usually late at night, even to the point of complaining that it woke them and disturbed their rest. Typically it stops as soon as people cross the threshold into the room.

Paul Klasky, of Boulder, Colorado, wrote on March 23, 2004, that back about a decade ago when at the Stanley, he heard piano

Photo taken January 18, 2004, after previous reports by staff of piano playing. Note the mist, orbs and ectoplasm. The pianist is presumed to be Flora Stanley.
Photo courtesy Chris Bechard / Alpenglow Media

music coming from the music room. When he looked in, he saw a young woman playing the piano. As he walked across the room to watch her, she suddenly turned into an old lady, then disappeared.

June 26, 2002, Marty and Madison Casey were sitting with Seamus Berkeley, attending the Rocky Ridge Music Center "Music in the Mountains Concert Series" in the Music Room. Shortly after intermission, while the trio was playing Schumann's Piano Trio in D-Minor, Op. 63, the sky turned suddenly very dark and the wind picked up. It blew so vigorously, it blew a window in the music alcove shut with a slam, startling everyone, though not to the point of stopping the highly skilled musicians.

At that moment, Marty and Seamus noticed a form, standing, then visibly moving to the left, outside the window that slammed shut. The presence of such a form outside that window was odd enough—the Music Room is a story above ground, with no place for standing outside those windows. Seamus and Marty both followed the direction to the left of the alcove, and caught the image of Flora through the glass porch doors, standing for just a moment before she slipped away from sight, upon which the wind stopped and the sky lightened back up, as suddenly as it had darkened.

After the concert, violinist Roy Malan came up to Marty and asked her what had happened. Although not showing any reaction to the obvious weather disturbance, the musicians had watched Marty's and Seamus's faces and knew something else was happening. As you remember, Marty was the Stanley Museum site manager in 1998 who first started the Ghost Story Tours at the hotel. She knew Stanley history, and knew well what Flora looked like.

Photo taken January 18, 2004, in the mirror in the Piñon Room after previous guests and staff reported brief images being seen. Ectoplasm next to Chris appears to be a cowboy.   *Photo courtesy Chis Bechard / Alpenglow Media*

PIÑON ROOM

The Piñon Room is known as the gentleman's smoking room, which fits the real wood in this room, contrasting with the plaster, now fake wood, in the Lobby and the MacGregor Dining Room. In the history of the hotel, this room has had many uses, from the smoking room to an ice cream parlor in the 1950s. This is also the room the ABC series used for the bar scene in its version of *The Shining*. Most sightings in this room are of images in the mirror, captured usually by digital cameras.

13

People staying in the east wing of the big hotel have told stories of hearing cars drive up on gravel, with the distinctive slam of car doors and the noise of a party going on the east porch next to the Piñon Room. When commenting about it to front desk clerks the next day, they were told there had been no party happening outside the Piñon Room, or anywhere else on the property, for that matter. They then realized that the parking lot of the Stanley is paved now, so there would be no sound of cars on gravel.

August 17, 2000, a guest saw F.O.'s face appear and disappear in the mirror during a tour. Most sightings have been in photographs.

F.O. Stanley playing pool in the Billiard Room, c. 1915.
Photo by Fred P. Clatworthy, from the Stanley Museum archives

BILLIARD ROOM

This room represents a key part of the grand resort aspect of the Stanley Hotel. On-site entertainment and amenities define grand resort, even to this day. In addition to billiards here in the main building, Stanley also had a full-size bowling alley in the basement of the Concert Hall / Casino. Stanley himself was an avid, and accomplished, game player, whether billiards or bowling, board games or word games and puzzles.

Sometime in the winter of 1983, Mark Lorenz, then working in Engineering and living in the hotel, was on his way to one of the only places on the property that had a TV in those days, the Executive Suites, now called Heritage Suites, behind the Billiard Room. He was walking through the right side of the double French Glass swinging doors when it swung barely six inches and abruptly stopped as if it had hit a person standing on the other side.

At that time the glass doors were covered with black-out curtains, so a view through was not possible. Thinking there was someone on the other side, Mark stopped pushing on the door and apologized for bumping into what he assumed to be a person. When there was no response, and a quick glance through the swinging door crack showed there to be no one on the other side, Mark stepped through the left hand door into the hallway, figuring something was stuck in the hinge of the right hand side. One stride later he stopped, sensing something was amiss.

The end of the hall showed a pile of drifted snow by the crack of the exterior door, a sign of cold hallway temperatures. No surprise there—he'd been working on getting heat into the rooms off that hall, and was fully aware the hall was not heated. But he was standing in a very warm space, completely incongruent with his knowledge—and with the snow, proof—that the hall was cold. He took a sideways step to the right and it was immediately as cold as it should be. By this time really confused, Mark raised his arm to feel the warm space he had just vacated, to confirm his experience. As if synchonized with his arm, the door, which had since come to rest, abruptly swung away from him, and the warm presence was gone.

Sometime in 2003, housekeeper Marie was cleaning rooms in the Heritage Suites behind the Billiard Room. As she walked across the hallway between rooms, she happened to look down the stairs through the swinging doors, at this time not covered with the darkening curtains, into the Billiard Room. There on the bench sat an old lady in a blue dress. Marie looked again, but the woman had disappeared. Trembling, Marie went directly to the housekeeping office in a panic and told Charlotte Riley, the head housekeeper, that she had seen a ghost—the lady in blue—and that the lady had looked at Marie as if looking though her. The look had given her chills. It took a while for Charlotte to calm her down.

SECOND FLOOR

The most famous room in the Stanley Hotel is without doubt Room 217 at the southwest corner of the second floor. Made famous most recently by Stephen King, it is also the room given Molly Brown of Titanic fame, and other notables.

Room 217

To provide the historic background, June 1911, this room was the site of a disaster. A storm had put the Stanley power plant out of commission, so the hotel went to its backup acetylene system. When Elizabeth Wilson, the chief chambermaid, came into 217 to light the lamp, the gas line in that room had apparently been on for some time, and the candle sparked an explosion. The ceiling and several heavy steel girders fell. Mrs. Wilson was hurled into the dining room below, sustaining two broken ankles. Four waiters were also injured. Damage was estimated at $50,000-$60,000 to the entire southwest end of the hotel (Longmont Ledger, p. 37). Mrs. Wilson's hospital bills were paid by Stanley, and she returned to her job after she healed.

Mrs. Wilson's gratitude to Stanley is thought by some to explain the "easy doors" and other happenings reported from 217 and in that wing of the hotel. Staff members have reported seeing a woman dressed as a chambermaid wearing old fashioned clothing in the area. Museum site manager Ellie DeLeone took a group to see the room one day and was so alarmed by the door first opening, then closing, that she refused to take tours to the room after that.

Other stories of room 217 include the appearance to staff and guests of a dark circle on the floor near the spot of the 1911 explosion. Some claim to have seen a face in the door. The light in the bathroom is located in an awkward spot, but often turns on by itself for guests.

Apocryphal stories abound of bags being packed while people are at breakfast the day they are to depart, of clothes having been straightened during the night while guests slept. The real magic of room 217 may exist in the personal experiences of the many couples who choose to spend their honeymoon there.

West Stairs, near 217

On April 18, 2004, Elizabeth and John Whisler of Aurora, Colorado, stayed at the Stanley Hotel for their honeymoon, checking out the next day. Elizabeth had had previous experiences with supernatural forces, but nothing as bad as what happened this time. She talked her husband into walking the evening ghost tour of the hotel. The tour was going fine and she was learning a lot when they approached the west end stair well on level Two. The tour guide, her husband and three other people walked across a spot where Elizabeth, however, stopped.

As she stopped, several of the tour guests heard what sounded like the pop heard when someone experiences static shock. The guests and guide turned around to see what happened and reported that Elizabeth's hair was standing straight up as if she had touched a static orb. She felt as though she had walked through a bubble that was popped by cold air. As the tour ended, she started to get a very painful headache that started making her sick. The next day after taking stuff out to the car, she talked her husband into going back to the spot again. As they approached the spot, John walked through it and Elizabeth followed where she was again popped with a static shock.

Room 219

In room 219, a guest once complained of opening a window, only to have it shut, and an opposite window open, seemingly on its own.

Room 222

In September of 2000, guests complained of noises in the room above, only to be told there was no-one booked in the room above.

Room 224

Upon arrival at the Stanley Museum from the Maine office, I was sitting on a bench while staff waited on customers. A man came to the counter to deliver a message. He spoke of being on the Ghost Story tour the night before, and he had something to report. I started thinking he had a complaint about the tour.

The man proceeded to tell how he and his wife had gone to their room after the tour, and had been trying to get to sleep. Noise from a party next door made it difficult. Worse than that, however, were the pillows—they were new, fat and hard, unlike softer ones his wife preferred.

After struggling with the noise and the pillows, they were finally drifting off to sleep, when they heard a knock on the door. They ignored it at first, thinking it must be for the group next door. But it persisted, until the man got up, went to the door and looked through the peep hole. As he did, he watched a bellman turn away and start walking down the hallway.

The man went back to bed, when suddenly the knock, now a bang, was back. This time the man jumped out of bed, went to the door to see that the bellman had returned, and opened it. "What do you want?" he asked the bellman with a touch of annoyance in his voice, to which the bellman replied, "Sir, didn't you order a soft pillow?" They had made no call for a pillow.

Room 234

October 6, 2001, a honeymoon couple staying in room 234 was subjected to bagpipers practicing in the room next door for a wedding. Oddly, they played "Amazing Grace," more a funeral than a wedding song. That night, when the husband sat down on the bed to write in his journal, the bed collapsed, two legs sawed off, and a third cut through on the other side of the bed. They had taken the Stanley Museum's ghost story tour that evening, and their tour guide, Diego, had primed them to accuse Dunraven. The front desk called Engineering, and the man who answered the call was mystified, but gave them from the Presidential Suite a wooden-leg bed, which did not collapse. This same couple had their picture taken later at Baldpate Inn, which showed a ghost in the picture where they should have been.

March 12, 2002, Darlene Wilson reported to Maureen Corey by email something that happened to her in September of 1989. A girlfriend from out-of-state came to visit her in Lakewood, Colorado. They decided to spend the night in Estes Park, and chose the Stanley Hotel. They got a twin double room and after dinner and talking, got to bed around 1 a.m.

Attributing it to being intuitive, Darlene "felt" the presence of a ghost, a young boy, wearing rompers, jumping up and down on the bed in the room above theirs. When her friend, Linda, turned out the light, the young boy jumped off the bed, came through the floor (the women's ceiling) and into Darlene's body from the back. She was on her side, facing the wall and was a bit frightened but didn't know what to do...other than to get her friend Linda to turn on the lights.

When she said Linda's name, it came out very deep and gravely and was something like... "LLLLLiiiiiinnnnnnnddddddaaaaaaaaaa."

Linda responded, "Darlene?" and again I said her name, "LLLLLLiiiiiinnnnnnnddddddaaaaaaaaaaa." She asked if Darlene wanted her to turn on the light, and Darlene responded, "Yyyyyeeeeeesssss."

When Linda turned on the light, the spirit left her body through the front so quickly that the whole bed was shaking. Linda then said, "Do I want to know what just happened?" and Darlene said, "No." They left the lights on for the rest of the night.

She "felt" that the boy was very young, around 6 years old, and that he died around something like 1912.

Six years later, when visiting Estes Park again, Darlene met some of her family at the Stanley Hotel for drinks. Her sister-in-law left to take a tour of the hotel on which she heard all about the hauntings of the Stanley. While she was away on the tour, Darlene shared her experience with her brother. On the sister-in-law's return from the tour, she started talking about the ghost of a little boy who wears rompers and loves playing tricks on people.

Room 202

October 15, 2001, two women, one a psychotherapist and one a life coach, were staying in room 202. Before retiring, the window rattled suddenly, then stopped. They did not hear it again all evening.

Around 2 a.m., they were sleeping when the lights turned on. Soon after, they heard what sounded like a "cart with square wheels" thumping loudly down the halls. They also heard a young girl giggling as she ran down the hall. In the morning, they discovered an old-fashioned hairpin on the bathroom floor.

One woman was on oxygen. Her oxygen tank had been full when she brought it in from the car. In the morning, it was inexplicably empty. Neither woman had known the hotel was haunted. Both wore really large crystals around their necks.

THIRD FLOOR

Third Floor Hall

There are frequent stories from night watchmen of doors not closing on this floor.

One was doing his rounds on the third floor. He checked each room for closed and locked windows, lights off, and to be sure everything else was in order. He completed his check of one particular room, and as he walked away from the locked room, the door opened. "Maybe it's one of those 'easy' or fussy doors," he thought to himself. He went back, looked in the room to verify the windows were indeed shut, closed and locked the door again. As he walked away, the door opened again. By this time he was getting annoyed, so he went back, checked again, and this time as he turned to leave and lock the door, a

Photo taken January 18, 2004, in main corridor of third floor, after previous guest reports of knocking on doors. Note mist / ectoplasm of possible culprit.
Photo courtesy Chis Bechard / Alpenglow Media

rush of cold air caught him. Enough of this, he thought to himself, shut the door and left, the hair standing up on the back of his neck.

Another night watchman doing his rounds tried in vain to close and lock the fire escape door at the end of the west wing corridor. Each time it opened, he returned, locked it, only to have it open as soon as he turned away. Finally, he gave up, and as he walked down the hall, the door closed with a bang, and locked on its own. The watchman, familiar with ghostly shenanigans, smiled—perhaps in defense of the hair rising on his neck—and continued walking.

Room 307

People staying in room 307 saw lights shining into room 201 on the floor below them. When they asked the front desk about the rooms, they were told there was no-one staying in 201 that night.

Room 317 — 417

Bartender Jason Kurtis was called to deliver ice to room 317. When he got to the door and knocked, a man answered the door and responded in a surly voice, "What do you want?" "Here's the ice you ordered, sir," Jason responded politely. "I didn't order any ice," the man snapped, and slammed the door shut. Jason returned to the bar, scratching his head about this one.

When he got back to the bar, the call came in again, "Where's my ice?!" Jason figured he'd gone to the wrong floor. So he took the ice to 417 and was greeted by the same man with the same surly response. At this point, Jason's skin got cold and clammy.

Room 318

Sometime in November 2003, while Dawn, the housekeeper, was cleaning room 318, she felt like she was being watched. She looked but no one was around. She went back to her cleaning and again felt like she was being watched, and this time looked toward the closet. She tried to ignore it and continued cleaning the room. She looked again and saw a see-through image of a woman standing just inside the closet. The spirit appeared to be wearing a long striped dress (either gray and white or blue and white) with a white high neck and long sleeved shirt, and a white apron. Her hair was pulled up into a bun.

Dawn thought her mind just imagined this until a week later when two women asked her about ghosts. One of the women did not believe, but the other swore she had seen a ghost in room 318 in the closet doorway. When she described the ghost, Dawn simply smiled and replied, "Yes, I saw her last week."

Other guests have reported strange things in 318. One boy felt something tapping on his chest. Another saw the pages of a book turn by themselves.

Another guest in this room, a man, felt the mattress on his bed begin to rotate counter clockwise. He was so upset, he drove back to Fort Collins at 11:30 that night rather than stay at the hotel.

Photo looking down the main corridor on the fourth floor. Room 401, a popular wedding suite and source of many stories, is off this hall. Note the mist and orbs.

Photo courtesy Chris Bechard / Alpenglow Media

Photo taken January 18, 2004, looking up at the entrance to the tower, where voices of a little boy had been heard that evening. This stairway, which is always locked today, is said to be an area where the children loved to play hide and seek, so the energy seems to be happy.   Photo courtesy Chris Bechard / Alpenglow Media

Room 340

Two young girls staying in room 340 were watching TV. Although sure they were alone, the bathroom door suddenly slammed shut, and they heard the door bolt.

THE FOURTH FLOOR

The fourth floor of the Stanley tells the most tales of hauntings on the entire Stanley Hotel property. In the early days of the hotel when families would come for the whole summer with children and staff, the private staff would stay on the fourth floor. Nannies would care for children here when the parents were busy. Family life was not child-centered then as it is today. "Children should be seen and not heard" was the mantra, and it extended to feeding the children in a windowless dining room off the kitchen, rather than at the assigned table with assigned staff in the elegant MacGregor Dining Room.

In February of 2004, housekeeper Dawn was asked to inspect rooms on the fourth floor that had recently had work done on them by the Engineering Department. *The Shining* was playing on the TV in the first, then the second and then the third room she went into. Her first thought was that Engineering had turned the TVs on, but Engineering never turns TVs on. She checked a fourth room and again the TV was on, again playing *The Shining*.

At this point, Dawn was called to take care of something on another floor. She deliberately turned off the TV, and closed the door, not realizing she had left her rooms check list behind. When she returned to the fourth floor, she checked two more rooms, which also had their TVs on, then realized she did not have her list, returned to the room she thought she had left the list in, and the TV, which she had so deliberately turned off—witnessed by another housekeeper—was on again.

She then looked up and down the hallway, and said out loud, "Okay, that's it. Stop playing with the TVs!" She didn't encounter another TV turned on for the rest of the day. After this, she told the

Photo taken Januray 18, 2004, in West Hallway of the fourth floor, where repairs were underway. The engineering department had reported that items kept being moved throughout the hallway when the men were not present.

Photo courtesy Chris Bechard / Alpenglow Media

spirits that they needed to leave her alone, and it seems they did—mostly.

Other guests staying on the fourth floor hear furniture moving overhead during the night. The fourth is the top floor, however; there are no rooms above.

Both Stanley Museum tour and hotel guests have sensed spirits moving in clusters, documented by repeated photos. Others have reported a green mist moving back and forth across the hallway.

Room 401

The week of June 16, 1996, Rev. Kimberly Henry and her husband came to spend the week of the summer solstice at the Stanley. It turned out that Rev. Henry knew the Head of Reservations, Karen Lynch. Since they were staying for a week, Rev. Henry thought a room on the fourth floor would be best, so Karen arranged for the couple to stay in room 401. After the first couple of days, Rev. Henry reported to Karen that she kept smelling cherry-flavored pipe tobacco. Karen was mystified, explaining that Room 401, also one of the hotel's choice honeymoon suites, was a non-smoking room.

The third night, Rev. Henry reported to Karen that they had both seen a ghost standing in the corner of the room next to the closet, watching them. She described the spirit as a man who was bald on the top of his head with a distinct ring of hair around the bold spot.

She also reported that at one point, her husband had been next to the sink, put his wedding band down on the sink, and it mysteriously swept into the sink and down the drain. The couple called the front desk who called Engineering who rescued the ring. Another time, the husband had put his glasses down on the table, and they suddenly flew onto the floor, as if someone had swept them off the table. During the course of the week, it was clear to both of them that the spirit did not like the man, because it didn't do anything to annoy the woman during that time, beyond his appearance.

The two friends had talked of getting together for lunch, so on the fourth day the couple came downstairs at noon to join Karen, whom they met at the front desk. Karen's reservation office was behind the front desk, in a room that had a door to the hallway that connected the Dunraven Bar and Grille on the one side, and the MacGregor Dining Room on the other, so Karen went out through her office to meet them in the hallway to go to the restaurant. The

Windham Thomas Wyndham-Quin, the fourth Earl of Dunraven, some-times thought to haunt room 401. From his portrait next to the MacGregor Dining Room.   *Stanley Museum photo*

couple walked through the lobby toward the restaurant corridor, and as Karen came out her door to meet them, the woman suddenly gasped and fell to her knees, pointing to the picture of Dunraven hanging on the wall in the hallway next to the MacGregor. "That's the man! That's the man I saw in my room!" The husband reached over and helped his wife to her feet, while Karen stood dumbfounded at the woman's reaction, and more convinced than ever of her stories.

Several years later, when Karen's office was in the Manor House, she was called over to the Lobby of the main building to talk with two women who wanted to talk about ghosts. The front desk often called Karen when people wanted to talk of spirits. When she got to the Lobby, she met a woman and her daughter who wanted to know about any ghosts in the building. Karen started to respond, when the daughter told her there were six ghosts standing right here, and she pointed to the door of the MacGregor Dining Room. The women brought Karen over toward the door, and told Karen to stand in one particular spot. Karen said no way, she wasn't going to stand where there was a ghost.

The women gave up trying, but not before they told Karen that the woman standing in that spot was particularly beautiful, but very sad. She was apparently love struck by someone on the stage. Karen thought that was strange, since at that point there was no stage there.

Karen then told them the Dunraven story, to which the young girl said, "Let's go upstairs to the fourth floor, and we'll get him to leave." Karen thought this would be interesting, so she called her friend, Carrissa Delisse, from the front desk, and Karen got the elevator and took everyone to the fourth floor. Room 401 is next to the elevator, so Karen left the elevator door open. The young woman told them all to hold hands and close their eyes. That was too much to ask Karen and Carrissa, so they peeked while the young woman spoke: "Lord Dunraven, this is not your place, you must go now."

Suddenly a strong wind came right up the elevator shaft, and Karen, Carrissa and the mother all reacted with shudders. The young woman still had her eyes shut, and Karen said to her, "Did you feel that?" Opening her eyes, the young woman responded, "What?" All three woman responded almost in unison, "You mean you didn't feel that," to which she again responded, no she had not felt anything.

So what is the story of Lord Dunraven? Irishman Windham Thomas Wyndham-Quin, the fourth Earl of Dunraven, came to Estes Park in December of 1872, acquired more than 6,000 acres of land, and left Estes Park for his home in Ireland for the last time in the early 1880s. He eventually sold his land in 1908 to the partners F.O. Stanley and Greeley resident, Burton D. Sanborn. Stanley immediately carved a 180-acre piece out of the holdings to build his new hotel.

Stanley and Dunraven trusted each other sufficiently that Stanley was content to break ground for his new hotel in June 1907, a full year before the land deal was signed June 16, 1908. Perhaps it was that sense of trust that encouraged Stanley to plan on naming his hotel

The Dunraven.

Estes Park townspeople were not pleased, however, and in October 1908 presented Stanley with a petition:

> *"Mr. Freeland (sic) O. Stanley, Greeting: We the undersigned, appreciating the good work you have done in Estes Park, hereby petition that the building which will stand as a monument to its founder, shall be called "The Stanley Hotel."*

To think that Dunraven roams the Stanley Hotel at all, one can only surmise that it is out of gratitude for Stanley's attempt, at least, to name the hotel for him. He was known to like women, however, so it would not be unusual that he hang around the honeymoon suite, nor that he show disdain for the bridegrooms and husbands.

In October 2002, Mr. and Mrs. Andrew Smith of Thornton, Colorado, recorded on their video camera through the windows of room 401 what he was sure were ghosts in room 407. White forms in the window were not visible at all with the naked eye, but were through the camera with night vision. After many viewings, there appeared to be a child on the bottom half and a larger form above it. One could make out the arms and the legs of the child in the bottom portion of the glass. It appeared as if a person were walking and a "hand" were coming out from the left side, then the form disappeared.

Immediately after watching this, the Smiths called the front desk and the accommodating staff took them into the unoccupied room to get some pictures. After seeing the room, they noticed that there couldn't possibly be a person in the position that the "forms" were in because the bathroom sink was immediately below the window. Not only would the person need to be six feet tall, he or she would have to have been double jointed.

Room 404

November 20, 2003, two women staying in room 404 were getting ready to go out to town when they heard laughter in the hallway. They didn't think anything about it, but did stop by Safeway on their way home to buy a white candle to light to make the spirits leave them alone—or according to the mother of one of the women, attract the spirits.

As they are sitting and playing cards, the candle began to flicker intensely. One of the girls asked the spirits to "cut it out," and the candle flickered yet more intensely. The women proceeded to watch a movie, and both of them heard the door knob begin to turn, as if someone were trying to enter the room.

A little later, both heard what they described as a buzzing noise, similar to the sound a car remote would make, coming from near the closet. The ladies had had enough by this time and called the front desk and requested to switch rooms. The buzzing sound became louder as the lady called the front desk. They were moved to room 201

Mist showing in pictures, on a perfectly clear night, and where none appeared in an earlier picture.
Photo courtesy Will and Ann Rice

and nothing more happened.

Room 405

Staff and the occasional guest reported music blaring for days from this room. No-one was staying there.

Room 406

December 11, 2004, at 8:45 p.m., Will and Ann Rice, visiting from Pittsfield, IL, took pictures in the inner courtyard of the Stanley from the top of the stairs near the Cascade Waterfall, up toward their room, 406, on the fourth floor of the hotel. The third image in their digital camera showed a misty form clearly not there in the first two images. The evening was clear and calm, so the mist could not be tied to weather. That evening around 11:30, they began to hear sounds of

Photo taken January 18, 2004, on the fourth floor in the west hallway, where guests and staff previously reported sounds of running children.

Photo courtesy Chris Bechard / Alpenglow Media

running in the hallway outside their room, despite being the only guests in that wing. The sounds continued throughout the night, no voices, only footsteps running.

In Summary

In June 2004 Tom Danton was having lunch at the Sundeck Restaurant in Estes Park when several old friends dropped in and sat at the table next to him. They hadn't seen each other in months, so they asked what he was doing these days. Tom mentioned that he worked at the Stanley Museum at the Stanley Hotel and conducted History and Ghost Tours there. Just as he said that, a waitress came out of the swinging door behind him with a full tray of food.

When she heard Tom say the Stanley Hotel and Ghost Tours, she gasped. She quickly distributed her dishes at a nearby table, then came over to Tom's table.

"You work at the Stanley?" she said very excitedly. "I'll never go back near that place again!" she exclaimed. "The ghosts are just too annoying there."

She went to explain that during the summer of 2001, she worked in housekeeping for three months at the Stanley Hotel, and nearly every day was another paranormal experience.

When cleaning guest rooms, she would often discover that right after she finished a room, the lights would come back on, the windows would open (after she closed them), and sometimes the impression of a body on the bed would reappear as soon as she smoothed it out. She did not appreciate having to do her job twice or more in the same room.

In the dormitory, she had an upstairs room on the north side. Every night she would lock her door and lay out her shirt, her hair brush, and other items she would need first thing in the morning so that she could get dressed in a hurry. Come morning, her door was still locked, but the items she had set out were all gone. She never "lost" anything. She might find her brush in the kitchen, her shirt in the bathroom, and other items scattered in other public areas of the dormitory. These morning searches were an annoying, not to say disturbing, way to start her mornings.

Aware that old buildings have door keys that often fit more than one door, she went to Ace Hardware and bought a sliding bolt which she installed on her door. Even then, her clothes disappeared, clearing her fellow staff of the crime. She finally gave up putting out her clothes because she spent too much time looking for them.

The scariest situations that she encountered would happen if she woke up in the middle of the night. She would see shadow-type people walking on the walls of her room. This really scared her. She would roll up in a ball in the middle of the bed and hide under her covers, too scared to open her eyes again until dawn.

As she told her stories, she was visibly shaken just remembering these incidents. She also said that many of the housekeepers had similar experiences. She was thrilled and relieved when her three month commitment to the hotel was up and she could get away from the Stanley. She refuses even to set foot on the property again.

In the early 1990s, a team of psychics was brought in to evaluate the hotel. They did determine that there were indeed spirits in the hotel, and that they were benign. Years later, a hotel staff person saw one of the psychics at an event elsewhere, and asked why she had never come back, since the spirits were pleasant and harmless. She answered, "Yes, but there are so many of them, they jumble up my mind!"

Photo taken January 18, 2004, in the main fourth floor corridor, looking up at the ventilation grate. Chris noticed the grate vibrating prior to taking the photo.
                                        Photo courtesy Chris Bechard / Alpenglow Media

THE TUNNEL AND SERVICE BUILDINGS

Here we will discuss the Stanley property as a whole, starting in its foundation, the much-touted Tunnel.

The Tunnel

Many hope that the Tunnel is the source of hauntings, perhaps left over from *The Shining*. As we know, the spirits at the Stanley Hotel have returned from the halcyon days of long, carefree summers, when the Tunnel didn't exist in today's form—it was not dug out until 1983 when the hotel was insulated, central heat was put in, and the hotel became a year-round resort. It is interesting to note that there was no foundation as we think of it today, that the building was simply laid on the ground, shimmed to the rocks it sits on. This reflects its summer season nature. Only later was it dug out, as space was needed, and summer resorts sought to extend its business into the "shoulder seasons," spring and fall, of the year.

The West Side

Just as the Billiard Room tells a part of the Grand Resort story, so do the buildings to the west of the hotel. As resort hotels were virtually self-sufficient entertainment centers, so were they self-sufficient with staff, maintenance, even food, often having gardens. Although the Stanley Hotel did not have its own produce gardens, it did have its own ice pond for its iceboxes and food preparation. The ice pond can still be seen on the curve of the service road below the old generator building used today as an occasional stable.

Staff Dormitories

Staff buildings to the west housed black and white staff at first, today men and women, separately. Stories abound of employee's things going lost, to be found the next day in strange locations. Perhaps some can be attributed to mischievous spirits, some to mischievous staff.

Power Plant

The old generator building below the former laundry, today's Engineering Department, has been used for a stable from time to time. Although there have been no horses there for some time, staff still reports hearing and smelling them.

The Manager's House

Today the Executive Offices, the old Manager's House, has reported only one spirit. F.O. Stanley is occasionally seen looking over the shoulders of the staff managing his property.

Presidential Suite/Former Gate House

This building was originally the gate house, located well below the hotel near today's intersection of US Routes 34 and 36, about in the parking lot where the Egg & I now sits. The road swept up through the meadow, on the east side of today's Safeway supermarket in Stanley Village. It was moved to its present location so long ago, no one seems to remember when it happened. Over the years, it has served many functions, from staff housing to offices. Today it is called the Presidential Suite.

On December 4, 2003, Mr. and Mrs. Derek Key, Austin, Texas, and Mr. and Mrs. John Craigmile, Buda, Texas, were staying here. At 10:30 p.m., the couples bolted the front doors shut and retired to bed. Derek heard footsteps in the kitchen and near the first-floor bedroom. Around 4:30 a.m., Mrs. Key heard a man and woman talking upstairs.

The next morning, the Keys asked the Craigmiles about having gone out again after they'd come in together. Mr. Craigmile was surprised. "I thought you guys went out again!"

Neither party had left their rooms after 10:30 p.m.

Today, the Stanley Hotel is a small hotel. In 1909, it was considered "simply palatial, equaling anything of its size in the world" (Rocky Mountain News, p. 50). As with guest ranches in Estes Park, people stayed for months, perhaps a reason for haunting.

To the left, on the west side of the hotel, hangs the balcony right outside room 217. Note that the building does not have shutters, sometimes mentioned when people try to dramatize King's inspiring night in the Stanley.

Next to the tower in the center of the building is the elevator machinery shaft. Unfortunately, it breaks the symmetrical lines typical of the eastern Georgian Colonial Revival style Stanley chose. Recently it has become even more noticeable, heightened to enclose a new, more powerful, motor for the recently restored elevator—a reminder that the Stanley Hotel is first and foremost a business, despite its placement on the National Register of Historic Places. The present ownership has spent millions bringing it back to its rightful place as an economic engine in the Town of Estes Park. The next three buildings, the Manor House, Concert Hall and Carriage House, complete the dramatic four-building sweep sited so sympathetically in its Rocky Mountain backdrop by its builder, F.O. Stanley.

This photograph illlustrates the artistic siting, sympathetic to the landscape behind.
From the Stanley Museum archives

MANOR HOUSE

The Manor House was completed and in service for the 1910 season. Stanley made allowances for the building by leaving a space for it, but he wanted to see whether business his first year would justify building it. A nearly-exact model of the larger hotel, it has 33 rooms today compared to the 99 in the main bulding. Sometime around 1916, Stanley expanded again, extending the east wings on both buildings and putting an extension on the wing of the Carriage House. If you look carefully, you can see where the additions occurred.

In the spring of 2001, Dawn, who later took a job as a house-keeper at the Stanley, came to the hotel to take photos. She got no further than the Manor House where she experienced the "echo" of a dance in the front banquet room, on the west side, the equivalent location of the MacGregor Room in the main hotel. She tried to cross the room, but as she got closer to the middle of the room, it got harder to walk in a straight line. It was like walking through people dancing. As she got closer to the window, it got easier to walk. She stood at the

35

window for a while, and decided the easiest way to leave the room was to walk along the edge.

She then walked to the third floor and suddenly felt very sad, almost to the point of crying. She felt a gentle push against her left shoulder while standing at the top of the stairs. She stepped down a couple steps and stopped. Again, she felt the push against her shoulder. She whispered, "OK, I'm leaving now." The push then stopped and she left.

She ended up with photos of distinct images of spirits in windows and mirrors that made believers out of skeptics. Those photos traveled through so many hands that she doesn't know where they are, and it was a year before she set foot back on the property again.

January 5, 2002, guests held a seance in room 1209. In the middle of the night, a man with a top hat floated by with his knees up. In room 1214, guests have reported a chair appearing out of nowhere in the middle of the room, and of keys bending sideways in the door. Several housekeeping and engineering staff have seen a red spot on the floor in the same place in the basement.

As guests have reported in the main hotel, people on the top, in this building the third, floor, have reported hearing bellmen above them, when there is no floor above the third floor in the Manor House.

Arty Roberts, who has been a housekeeper for years at the Stanley, tells of meeting Mrs. Stanley on the stairs of the Manor House. One of Arty's most repeated spirit sightings was of the Lady in Green, whose identity became known to her in yet another incident in a restroom in the Concert Hall.

While cleaning the Ranch Room at the Manor House—the equivalent room to the Piñon in the main building—Arty happened to glance up the hallway to see a lady in a green dress standing in the doorway of the last room on the corridor. The dress went to the woman's mid-calf. Her pretty, and very white, face was framed by short hair and a broad-brimmed green hat. Most remarkable was the smell of her lovely perfume, a smell Arty noticed every time she cleaned in that part of the Manor House.

THE CASINO OR CONCERT HALL

Most stories about the Casino, now called Concert Hall, come from staff. From being hit on the head with plaster—quite possible in recent years before being restored—to having trash strewn across the hall, the stories seem to bother staff more than many of the stories in the main building.

Long-time housekeeper Arty Roberts tells of being locked in the Men's Room. More frightening, and this time with a witness, Arty was cleaning the bathrooms in September 1994 when she felt her wrist being grabbed and her hand forced to write "Mary Donovan, Aug. 18, 1927" on the mirror. Arty had been chasing the identity of the Lady in Green for some time; she was convinced Mary Donovan was the name of the Lady in Green.

Another woman in the cleaning crew noticed that the roof of the Casino would be black with ravens when she went to clean it, and they would all fly off when she left.

Stanley buildings from old brochure.   *From the Stanley Museum archives*

The Carriage House

The only story that seems to come out of the Carriage House, still sadly unrestored, is of a major party there in December 1994, seen by both a cook and a guest. There was no party.

F.O. Stanley Home

Although no spirits have been experienced at the Stanley home by Gary and Kelly Brown, the present owners, they do tell stories of their Carriage House. When the Browns first moved to Estes Park from Denver, Judge Brown's secretary, Joyce McCulley, came with them, and from 1983 lived in their guest house, the converted Carriage House, for several years. Stanley had not only kept his car there, he also had one of his famous garage turntables in it, so that he didn't have to back up. He also set up his workshop here, where he built violins and wooden toy guns for his young friends.

Joyce had been noticing strange things, and called over to the Browns, who let their dog out to make sure there wasn't a prowler. The dog got quite excited, but no-one found any indication of a prowler. This happened again later, until Joyce stopped letting it concern her. One night, as she lay in bed, she looked up to see a man approach the foot of her bed. Inexplicably, she was not frightened. She suddenly recognized it to be F.O. Stanley. He spoke to her, "Are you all right?" She responded, "Yes, I am," to which he nodded, turned and disappeared. She was never disturbed or visited again.

In fact, Joyce was not well. She had breast cancer, from which she would die a few years later. Many of the Stanley stories we hear express care and concern, for guests, for friends. Ever the perfect host, Stanley was concerned and needed to be assured for himself. One can't help wonder what Stanley would have done if Joyce had said "No." As a spirit there is, after all, not much that he could have done. However, in real life, we know from history, he would have done everything in his power and pocketbook to fix it.

The Stanley Museum has been collecting ghost stories and spirit sightings since its arrival at the Stanley Hotel in 1997, and even past its departure in 2004, a full eight years of documentation. Truth be told, only one of the staff at the Museum ever experienced anything, including this author.

BIBLIOGRAPHY
Stanley Ghost Stories

Beahm, George. *The Stephen King Story: A Literary Profile.* Kansas City, Missouri: Andrews and McMeel, 1992.

King, Stephen. *Secret Windows: Essays and Fiction on the Craft of Writing.* New York: Book-of-the-Month Club, 2000. An exclusive Book-of-the-Month Club anthology of hard-to-find non-fiction pieces, little-known interviews, short stories, and articles about writing. Introduction by Peter Straub.

Lewis, James R. *The Death And Afterlife Book: The Encyclopedia of Death, Near Death, and Life After Death.* Canton, Missouri: Visible Ink Press, 2001.

Longmont Ledger, newspaper, June 30, 1911.

Rocky Mountain News, newspaper, June 13, 1909

Publisher's Afterword

In 1916, Wellesley College (Wellesley, Massachusetts) held an elaborate pageant to commemorate the tercentennial of the death of William Shakespeare. In the audience was a distinguished older gentleman, a man of science, culture and enterprise. He watched the actors, more than 300 in number, his favorite niece (a recent Wellesley alumna) among them, perform excerpts from the plays and poetry of the famous bard. The players eventually came to present a spirited performance of select scenes from *Macbeth*, depicting the play's many ghosts and witches as if they really existed. The old man grew increasingly uncomfortable, and finally, his patience spent, he rose and walked out of the performance with as much dignity as he could muster. He did not return.

The gentleman was Freelan Oscar (F.O.) Stanley. A native of Kingfield, Maine, he was back in Massachusetts at his Newton summer home, taking steps towards his retirement from the Stanley Motor Carriage Company. Since 1903, when he was diagnosed with a potentially terminal case of tuberculosis, he had spent most of his days on doctor's orders in the mountains of Colorado, at Estes Park. Industrious and active by nature, he coped with his medical exile by throwing himself into civic projects in his new home, building roads, power stations, waterworks, and vital infrastructure improvements.

In 1908, taking up an enterprise shared by other individuals of the day similarly displaced from their former homes and occupations, F.O. Stanley chose to further promote the area and its attractions by building a hotel. Not just any hotel – a grand hotel that would rival any of the great resort hotels in the White Mountains of the east where F.O. and his wife Flora spent many adventures while vacationing with their early motor car in the waning years of the 19th Century. The Stanley Hotel would become the centerpiece of F.O. Stanley's many contributions to Estes Park.

Fast forward to the present day. The Stanley Hotel, still grand and still in business, has become known as one of the most haunted hotels in the west. Thanks in part to a chance stay in 1974 by horror author Stephen King (by coincidence another famous Mainer) who was inspired to write his best-seller, *The Shining* (later filmed by another famed "Stanley," Stanley Kubrick), the hotel has come to be celebrated as a paranormal center *par excellence*.

Since King and Kubrick, stories of the hotel's haunting have proliferated, both collected and channeled by members of the hotel's staff, of whom it is estimated that fully 75% have experienced unexplained phenomena while at work. Stories abound of mysterious children running about unattended, of long-deceased chambermaids and restless guests roaming the halls. It is said that there have been sightings of the ghosts of Lord Dunraven (who originally established a private hunting preserve on the land on which the hotel sits) and F.O. Stanley (who bought and rescued the land for the good of the community). Perhaps the most celebrated paranormal spectre is F.O.'s wife, Flora Stanley, who is said to play her Steinway piano in the hotel's music room, only to disappear when the music attracts due attention.

Ghosts have become big business, generating much-needed income for cash-strapped hotels and run-down historic districts. Institutions which in the past would have shunned such activity have lately taken full advantage of the anti-science tenor of our times to embrace this supernatural revenue stream. The Stanley Museum of Kingfield, Maine, which once struggled to maintain a branch museum in Estes Park, is perhaps as guilty as any in this regard considering that the Museum once instituted its own popular "ghost tours" of the Stanley Hotel and published this book to promote them.

This is not to say that ghost stories do not have any benefit in our contemporary society. Recently, talented authors of young adult literature have used the characters of ghosts, vampires, witches, warlocks and other paranormal beings as allegories to sensitively address subjects of teen suicide, alienation, peer pressure, drug dependency, and even eating disorders – and these books (whatever one might say about their literary merit) have been found to have an admirable influence. Similarly, the trustees of the Stanley Museum hoped that the success of *Stanley Ghost Stories* would inspire historic interest in the true Stanley stories in Estes Park and what these stories can teach us today.

Sadly, this book falls short of these nobler expectations. Even a casual reading of these stories would find that they have been largely assembled, promulgated and passed along by those with a vested commercial interest in their tourist appeal. What historical facts there might be to substantiate these stories have been shunted aside, as such facts more often than not simply get in the way.

A case in point would be Flora Stanley. Born in 1847 on a rural farm in the village of Hartford, Maine, she would first make her mark as a gifted school teacher in the nearby town of Mechanic Falls where she met and married a fellow teacher, F.O. Stanley, in 1876. Her independence, resourcefulness and business acumen were considered remarkable for a woman of her day, and a source of pride for her husband. Her writings, letters and diaries are filled with wit and humor, and her social life was filled with dedication to civic service.

Flora was also courageous. In 1899, she accompanied her husband on the first successful motor climb of a major mountain, a risky ascent of the primitive Mount Washington Carriage Road in New Hampshire, in an early steam-powered Stanley Locomobile, seated above a high-pressure steam boiler wrapped with piano wire over a tiny inferno of burning gasoline. The mountain was famous for the worst weather ever recorded, and their motor carriage was known for flimsy tires and even flimsier brakes. It was not a venture for the faint of heart, and how they got down in one piece is still today a cause for some wonder.

The historic facts of this remarkable woman's life have been overshadowed and surpassed by the ersatz tales of her 'afterlife'. Browsing the internet for "Flora Stanley" will retrieve numerous references to the ghostly apparition disturbing the peace of paying guests at the Stanley Hotel with off-hours piano playing, and scarce mention of her exemplary character. In addition, the curse of being a female ghost inevitably gives rise to hints and suggestions of dark secrets and personal demons, as if women are more sensitive and prone to psychological disorders (a coin-toss in this case between *manic depression* and *bipolar disorder*) and thus haunted themselves – a proposition that is not only false but denigrating.

About that piano playing: while there are anecdotal stories of Flora Stanley playing her piano at the hotel for the entertainment of guests, there is no real evidence that she did so. F.O. Stanley knew that his wife, who grew increasingly blind with age, appreciated fine music, so he built an acoustically-designed music room, equipped it with a first-class Steinway, and hired professional musicians to give concerts for his wife to enjoy. It would seem that Flora the pianist is as much a myth as Flora the piano-playing ghost.

If the real Flora made for poor ghost material, her husband was far, far worse. F.O. Stanley was, in his own words, "always a confirmed skeptic," as was his twin brother, Francis Edgar (F.E.) Stanley. There are numerous well-documented accounts of the Stanley brothers' contempt for all things paranormal, which they dismissed in their fashion as "humbug."

In one noted example, F.O. writes about an 1893 incident at the Stanley Dry Plate factory in Watertown, Massachusetts, where the brothers needed a new well to successfully carry out their business, and the well-driller, to their dismay, showed up with a dowser. After a discussion with the contractor, the twins acquiesced to the dowser's services but insisted that he repeat his water-witching while blindfolded. According to F.O., the "blind test" proved the better of the dowser, who failed to repeat his results, although this failed to change the well-driller's mind, as F.O. ruefully notes.

The Stanleys did not shy away from taking on the more prominent exponents of the American Spiritualist movement and other quasi-scientific practitioners of their day. The Spiritualist movement, with its mediums, séances, ghostly specters, and interactive communication with the spirit world, was in many ways the early 20th Century parallel to the popular ghost investigations of today. Mrs. F.E. Stanley, in her diary entry for December 5, 1909, relates with some chagrin that when the Stanleys invited a prominent actor and spiritualist, Walter Hampton, to their house for dinner, he and her husband got into a "long argument" over "physic research."

In the *Newton Graphic* for January 2, 1903, F.O. Stanley went public with his beliefs by writing a scathing critique of what he considered to be the pseudo-scientific underpinnings of the Christian Scientist philosophy, taking his argument directly to the church's founder, Mary Baker Eddy, whom he challenged to take a winter's ride in his motor carriage, protected from frostbite by her faith alone. (She passed on the offer.) F.O.'s definitive opinion of spiritualism and the paranormal is best expressed in his own words, taken from a letter written to his wife, Flora, from Chicago on March 27, 1889:

> I have got some real news to relate. I went yesterday in company with a man whose acquaintance I have made here to have a sitting with a spiritualistic medium. You know I have always been a confirmed skeptic. There are several stopping at this hotel who are firm believers and we have had some interesting discussions on the subject. Well, to make a long story short we decided to submit our difference of opinion to a practical test. There is a Mrs. Bishop, who they claimed, could go into a trance and tell my family history better than I could myself. We went and I was completely convinced - that the whole thing was a humbug. You see if the lady had told the truth it would have certainly been miraculous for not one in the party knew a single fact of my past history. She told me my father was dead and my mother was living. [*In 1889, F.O.'s mother was deceased; his*

father was still living.] That I had two sisters living and one dead. [*F.O. had only one sister.*] That I was unlike all the other members of my family, in looks and character. [*F.O. had an identical twin brother and they shared many characteristics with their other siblings.*] My occupation that of a lawyer, and that I had an important case on trial which was going to terminate successfully. [*F.O. never studied law, and was not inclined to do so.*] That I had a friend by the name of George, one by the name of Charles, and another by the name of John. How wonderful! Such odd names. You will probably be very jealous when I tell you that I had a very intimate lady friend by the name of Martha. She said I was married and had three children. [*F.O. and his wife were childless.*]

After she had gone all through my history I said to her that when I came in I was a skeptic. Now I was convinced (that she was a humbug but didn't say so). That I would like to ask some questions about my business prospects. I stated that I had just invested heavily in land (lie number one on my part) and would like to know if the speculation would prove successful. "Why," she said, "did you tell me that you had just bought land? The Spirits told me that and I was just going to mention it. Your enterprises," she said, "will prove of great value. In fact you are to be a very rich man inside of six months!" My only opposition would come from a short thickset man with red hair, that she could see standing by my elbow. This man had crossed my path several times.

My only trouble during the entire sitting was to keep a straight face. You ought to have seen the fun I had with the believers when we got back to the hotel. You may be sure that I enjoyed it.

The author of this letter, a man who once walked out of a play depicting ghosts because he couldn't abide with what he was watching, would seem to be the last person to be caught dead (if you will pardon the expression) haunting any location, however benignly. He did, however, beat the odds – surviving his illness against expectations and living a life of good works to the age of 91. He built a grand hotel that still stands today. It's a good story, and he liked good stories.

This book contains quite a few additional stories. It is said that one of the more remarkable things about the Stanleys is that throughout their life and times they always remained true to their character. It is unlikely that they would believe these *Stanley Ghost Stories*. Should you, the reader, believe otherwise, then by all means stay true to your character. If you should follow the Stanleys' values instead, may your only trouble (as F.O. says) be to keep a straight face.

—*James Merrick, Archivist, Stanley Museum*

STANLEY MUSEUM PUBLICATIONS

The Stanley Steamer: America's Legendary Steam Car by Kit Foster (© 2004, Stanley Museum). $49.95 (Cloth). Also available in a leather bound limited edition.

Bravo, Stanley!: The Racing History of Stanley and the 1906 Stanley Land Speed Record by H. James Merrick (© 2006, Stanley Museum). $19.95.

The Genealogy of the "Locomobile" Steam Carriage, 1899-1904 by Donald L. Ball. (© 1994, Stanley Museum). $8.00.

The Stanleys: Renaissance Yankees, Innovation in Industry and the Arts by Susan S. Davis. (Exton, PA: The Newcomen Society of the United States, © 1997). $3.00.

A History and Tour of the Stanley Hotel, Estes Park, Colorado by Susan S. Davis (© 1999, Stanley Museum). $9.99.

Commemorative Program – Centennial of the First Auto up Mount Washington by Susan S. Davis (© 1999, Stanley Museum). $5.00.

Mr. Stanley of Estes Park by James H. Pickering. (© 2000, Stanley Museum). $19.95.

Stanley Ghost Stories by Susan S. Davis. (© 2005, 2012, Stanley Museum). $10.95

"We Will Try This Hill" - The Climb to the Clouds 1904-1905 by H. James Merrick (© 2004, Stanley Museum). $5.00.

Complete set of *Stanley Museum Quarterlies*, 1981 - 2012. Technical articles, family and business history, key individual profiles. 79 issues. $135.00.

Reflections on Transportation and Communication: An Evening with R. Buckminster Fuller edited by Susan S. Davis (© 1983, Stanley Museum). $1.50.

The Stanleys of Newton: Yankee Tinkerers in the Gilded Age by Karen H. Dacey. (© 2009, Stanley Museum). $29.95 (cloth), $19.95 (paperback).

The Old Table Chair by Chansonetta Stanley Emmons. Centennial Edition. (© 2009, Stanley Museum). $11.95.

The Stanley Family by Chansonetta Stanley Emmons. Reprint of 1916 Edition. (© 1993, Stanley Museum). $9.99.

One may order any of these books electronically through the Stanley Museum website at www.stanleymuseum.org (Museum Shop link) or by contacting the Museum office at:

40 School Street, P O Box 77, Kingfield, ME 04947
Tel. (207) 265-2729 — Fax (207) 265-4700
Maine@stanleymuseum.org

www.ingramcontent.com/pod-product-compliance
Lightning Source LLC
Chambersburg PA
CBHW060054050426

42448CB00011B/2451